To my children
—Micah, Jacob, Katie, and Lydia.
I love you with my whole heart!

CONTENTS

INTRODUCTION

Hi, my name is Trina, and I am a recovering people pleaser. My drug of choice was obsessing over others. I thought it was normal. I thought it was what I should do. It seemed admirable to try to help, fix, and save others. My counselor defined addiction as, "despite the consequences, one continues to make the choice." Despite the soul-killing consequences, I still made the choice to value, honor, and love others more than myself.

This is my soul-awakening story. To awaken is to realize something. I realized at my core I was afraid. I was scared to be alone, unwanted, and rejected. People pleasing was a coping mechanism. It is how I hid and protected myself. I share my story in hopes to normalize fear. Fear distorts things, but there is another way to live.

A Chinese proverb says, "The journey of 1,000 miles begins with a single step." A journey of awakening begins with the awareness that you may be betraying yourself by pleasing people. It can be challenging work to unearth your true self under the layers of life. It is challenging but important work. It is so important that in the holy scriptures, the greatest commandments are to love God and love others AS ourselves. It wasn't until I was an adult, after years of religious training in a strict

20 Characteristics of a People Pleaser

* Overly accommodating
* Walks on eggshells around others
* Plays the martyr
* Feels like you never get to do what you want
* Obsesses about others
* Agitated thinking
* Neglectful
* Passive-aggressive
* Avoids conflict
* Over gives
* Others tell you that you are too sensitive
* Overthinks
* Judgmental
* Has high expectations for self and others
* Afraid to speak freely
* Feels stuck
* Thinks everyone knows better
* Feels like no one ever listens
* Needs validation
* Avoids appearing needy

community, that I noticed that small word AS.

To overcome people pleasing is to acknowledge we have not loved ourselves as much as we have loved others. I am not talking about the stuck-up kind of love. The love I am talking about is when we honor, respect, and value ourselves as much as we do others.

"What if our only purpose in this lifetime is to heal from people pleasing?" another recovering people-pleasing friend asked. As we talked, we imagined what would be possible in our lives if we were more loving, kind, and compassionate toward ourselves.

This is a book about peace. Peace with myself. Peace with others. Peace with God. Along with peace, this book is about courage—the courage to accept ourselves and the person we were created to be.

For most of my life, I held to the belief that others were more important or valuable than I was. I was taught to put others first.

In 8th grade, I read a poem that made a big impression on me. It is called "How to Be Perfectly Miserable." The first two lines are: "Think about yourself. Talk about yourself." I desired to be a good Christian. I worked hard to avoid rocking the boat. I didn't want to cause any "storms," for fear I'd be judged for doing something wrong, being bad, or not being a good enough Christian. I wanted to be good, and so I took this poem to heart. I didn't want to be miserable, so in my undeveloped mind I reasoned, "It is better to give than to receive."

I don't disagree with serving and honoring others, but my giving to others was unhealthy and manipulative. I unconsciously kept people happy in order to have my needs for love and belonging met. I believed the lie that if I pleased others, my relationships would be better.

I hope that by sharing my story, you will feel less alone in your journey of healing. I have included excerpts from my journals and at the end of each chapter a Freedom Toolkit to help you break free from your people-pleasing habits, as well as poems I call "Heartplay." My healing journey is the hope I offer to you. I hope you see your story more clearly because your story *matters*. You matter. The world needs the true, magnificent you.

"Friendship is born at that moment when one person says to another, 'What! You too? I thought I was the only one.'"

—C.S. Lewis

STEP 1

Let that Should (S*#t) Go

"One does not discover new lands without consenting to lose sight of the shore for a very long time."
—*Andre Gide*

It was a windy day in March. I went to visit my 99-year-old grandmother. Sadly, days prior to my visit, she was diagnosed with cancer. Selfishly, I wanted her to live to attend a birthday bash we planned for her 100th birthday.

When I was getting dressed that morning, I looked in my closet and had a dialogue with myself about what I should wear to go see my beloved grandmother, perhaps seeing her for the last time. I was aware that my choice of clothing shouldn't matter, but I was even more aware that it *did*.

This pressure started when I was a young girl, and I would go to see my grandparents on Friday nights. My grandmother would give me a warm hug.

"Oh! You're not wearing an undershirt?" she'd ask while rubbing my back. "It's so cold."

I wanted her to say, "Katrina, it's wonderful to see you."

But instead, I felt her disapproval.

As a strong woman, I am still aware I want to avoid those feelings of disapproval. Her opinion matters to me. Yes, I want to respect my elders, but that morning I said to myself, *I need to let this go and be unapologetically myself.*

I dressed that cold morning with the intention of showing my grandmother my wildest side. I put on my ripped jeans and red leather jacket.

When I knocked on the door to her room, she was in the bathroom. When she came out, she pushed herself toward me in her wheelchair. We embraced and in her next breath she said, "Don't wear those. You are better than that!" referring to my holey jeans.

I felt like I was 10 again. The directives I received were:

A good girl wears undershirts.
A good woman doesn't wear holey jeans.

The story I told myself was that I needed to go back to the drawing board. The message I heard was: Let me define you.

One day, my counselor asked, "You are so hard on yourself. Who holds the measuring stick?"

In many of our families, social groups, and religious communities, there is a blueprint that says you should behave in a certain way. I have a long list in my mind of what it means to be a good girl, good wife, and good mother. The list holds me hostage, repeating, *I should. I should. I should.*

Stop shoulding on yourself, my inner wisdom screams. I hold myself to impossible expectations. Somehow, I have always believed that I would be more pleasing to God if I followed the blueprint. I felt I needed to prove, strive, and struggle to "earn my stripes." I feared disappointing God—and also other people.

For most of my life, I wanted to avoid uncomfortable feelings, the look of disappointment on other people's faces if I didn't do something they thought I should. I signed on to their discomfort. I felt anxious and responsible for how they felt about me. I thought that if I didn't do what they thought I should do, they would love me less. If someone was unhappy, I felt pressure to work harder to keep people happy.

Very early in life, I internalized the belief that I received love from God, family, and others only if I adhered to the blueprint. I feared if I strayed, I would become the outcast, the one who gets talked about and, in some circles, even shunned.

I understood that when one person makes a change, it affects the whole family system, which in turn makes other people question their beliefs and choices. Picture a mobile above an infant's crib: When you touch one part of the mobile, the whole thing moves. In my restrictive, religious Mennonite culture, being the same as everyone else was believed to be oneness, or unity. My perception was life was more harmonious if everyone believed the same thing and lived the same way.

In my life, my blueprint of shoulds felt like a straight-jacket.

List of Shoulds

* A good girl should not talk back to her parents.
* A good girl should help with dishes after a meal.
* A good wife should freeze food for the winter, even green beans that are overgrown.
* A good wife should iron her husband's shirts.
* A good wife should give her husband enough sex so he doesn't look at porn.
* A good mother should not screw up her children by leaving her marriage.
* A good mother should be available 24/7 to meet the needs of her children and spouse.

Your Freedom Toolkit

○ Life is all about choices. Trust the Divine is more concerned about who you are becoming rather than what you are doing. Choose who you want to become and make choices aligned with who you want to be. Are you becoming more loving, peaceful, and free?

○ Check your motives. Are you choosing to love or hoping to get love? People pleasers often look like they are loving and giving freely, but pleasing can be manipulative if you are seeking something in return such as validation or approval.

○ Pay attention to words like *must, ought, and should,* which keep one from living free. Who is holding the measuring stick of expectations in your life?

○ Stop seeking validation and approval from other people. At any moment, you can give yourself your own approval. Think or say to yourself, "It is great to be [fill in your name]! I have my own approval!"

○ Realize you *are* better than that. I've learned that being unapologetically myself is about allowing myself to act in a way that feels true and beautiful to me.

○ Notice when you feel jealous of someone or something. Feelings of jealousy can be a map guiding you to make choices that are more aligned with how you want to live.

○ Make a commitment to make a different choice and take action. Remember take small steps with safe people.

○ Pray: Divine, save me from all the good things you don't want me to do.

Reflections

- Create a list of what you've been told/taught a good woman should do. What items do you want to keep on this list?

- Create a second list and change each should to could. How can you make choices in life with more freedom?

- In what ways are you afraid of being too much? Too needy? Too controlling? Too stylish?

- In what ways do you shrink so others don't feel small?

- What do you feel when you are deemed not "good" in someone's eyes? What do you do when these emotions show up?

STEP 2

Love Yourself Back to Life

"Self-care is never a selfish act. It is simply good stewardship of the only gift I have, the gift I was put on earth to offer others. Anytime we can listen to true self and give it the care it requires, we do it not only for our-selves, but for the many others whose lives we touch."
—Parker Palmer

On a family trip to Epcot, I enjoyed an attraction called Monsters Inc. Laugh Floor. Near the stage is a laughter meter mounted to a rocket ship. As the characters onstage make the audience laugh, the gauge on the meter goes up. Once the audience laughs enough, the meter hits the top, and the rocket ship launches!

As I sat in the audience laughing with my family, which in turn made the rocket launch, it made me think of our love meters. We each have a love meter within us. When you love yourself, the gauge on your love meter goes up. Allowing others to love us and fill our love meters is a worthy endeavor, but loving ourselves first allows us to give more genuinely to others. We can love more fully when we are giving from a full love meter. Once you pour enough love into yourself, you take off—just like that rocket ship in Monsters Inc. Laugh Floor! As comedian Lucille Ball said, "When you love yourself, everything else falls in line."

As a people pleaser, when you love yourself, you can let go of trying to manipulate others to give you the love you desperately want from them. Cheryl Richardson, life coach and author of *Extreme Self Care*, says, "Self-love is extraordinary mothering of self in mind, body, and spirit." Many people pleasers are in fact extraordinary mothers, doing everything and anything for their children but giving themselves some of their own love and attention is challenging.

Loving yourself back to life is about giving yourself some of your own best energy, which in turn benefits everyone around you. You know the saying, "If mama ain't happy, no one's happy." Each act of extraordinary mothering toward yourself is like a drop in a teacup. Once you put in enough drops, the water in the cup overflows. When your "cup" is full, it flows over to everyone around you, and everyone in your life benefits from your self-love.

Like I wrote in the introduction, I'm not talking about loving yourself in a stuck-up, selfish way. Loving yourself back to life is about honoring, appreciating, and valuing your life as much and more as you value any other human life. It's not selfish. I believe the Divine knew the value of self-love, respect, and honoring ourselves when his followers were commanded to love their neighbors As themselves.

Five years ago, I had an "aha" moment when I realized I was taking care of myself by exercising and eating nutritious food so I would have the energy to take care of others. It was a worthy endeavor, but I also didn't value myself and do those things simply because I was worthy to be taken care of. I did them so I would have the energy to better serve others.

One way to love ourselves is to allow others to help.

As people pleasers, we crave love, yet we also repel it. People pleasers can have a difficult time accepting help and love from others. Because of this, it's even more important for us to honor and value ourselves by opening ourselves to face our own vulnerabilities and insecurities.

After my fourth child was born, I reached out to my mom and shamed and blamed her for not being there to help me.

"I didn't think you needed me," she said. "You always seem like you have it all together."

As a people pleaser, I struggled with pride, thinking I can do things on my own, no one can do "it" as good as I can, and I don't need anyone. Loving myself looks like asking others for help and opening myself to accept the love and help of others.

I believe that God *is* pleased when I balance loving myself with loving others. Accepting this belief, I have faith God looks on me and smiles—simply because I am alive.

Journal September 2018

I asked him to leave

It was the most loving thing I ever did

For him

For me

I never wavered

The words, "you need to leave" came from a deep place

I felt so certain it was the next best thing

I had to do

It didn't feel like love

How could it be love?

I just fucked up my life

Our life

Within a week, he was at

the unemployment office

looking for a job

My certainty cost him his job

Did it?

That was a story I told myself for a long time
I asked him to leave
I didn't think
About where he would live
Or the impact on our 4 young children
I just felt certain I loved myself and
I loved him to say
Enough is enough
A slow-growing, "soul-threatening" tumor
Was sucking the life out of our marriage
We needed treatment
The treatment plan: Radical Love
Love causes you to do crazy things
It takes courage
To love yourself as you love others
Love looks like
Kindness
Grace
Self-respect
Forgiving ourselves
Truth telling
Asking for help
Love happens in
Small moments
Big moments
Love is radical

Loving Yourself Heartplay

Love yourself back to life
To freedom
To peace
You will have more love than you can imagine
An unexpected benefit is you discover
Others begin to trust you more
As you show up more vulnerable
Express your needs
Ask for help
You will discover
Others don't always need you to be
The fixer
Helper
Savior
Others want to give to you, too
Let them
You have trained them to think
You don't need help
You were given two hands
One hand to give
The other hand to receive
Keep the flow of giving and receiving going
You will never regret the decision
To receive your own love
And the love of others

Your Freedom Toolkit

○ Ask yourself, *How can I be as loving to myself as I am to others? What if I was 5 percent more loving toward myself today? What would I allow myself to be, do, and/or have?*

○ Pause for a moment. Place your hand on her heart and say, "I love you, and I am listening."

○ Be your own need meeter. Don't rationalize what you need. Take action. Ask yourself, *What do I need?* It's much easier meeting other people's needs. What do *you* need? Listen to your own needs. Start with your physical needs. Are you thirsty? Hungry? Tired? Give yourself some of your own attention.

○ Move with ease. Try this mantra: *I allow myself to flow with ease today.*

○ Be compassionate toward yourself. Notice, don't judge anything you do today. Compassion and judgment cannot coexist.

○ Feelings are information. Feelings like sadness can tell us what we are missing. Identifying feelings can help us recognize our needs, wants, and desires. For example, *I am sad; I need reassurance. I am scared; I need comfort.*

○ Observe how you speak to yourself. Is it draining or uplifting? Speak to yourself like you speak to family and friends. Don't utter a word to yourself that you wouldn't say to a friend.

○ Be sensual. Elevate your experiences by engaging your senses. Do for yourself like a mother would do for her child or family: Draw a bath and add bubbles. Cover yourself with a fluffy blanket. Light candles at dinnertime or bedtime. Honor yourself by doing small acts of love for yourself.

○ Pray: Divine, help me to see the truth of who I am, no matter how beautiful it is.

Happiness Heartplay

If others are happy, then I am happy
What if I only kept myself happy?
What if I bring this back into balance?
It is tiring
It is not working
Stop initiating
Be in the hard pain of feeling lonely
Forgotten
Learn to make myself happy
No judgement
I can't take care of anyone right now
I need to care for myself
They never asked for my help
I thought they needed me to take care of them

Reflections

- In what ways can I be more like an extraordinary mother to myself?

- What loving thing can I do for myself today?

STEP 3

Kick FOPO (Fear of Other People's Opinions) to the Curb

"Care what others think and you will always be their prisoner."
—Lao Tzu

Coloring in the lines traumatized me.

It's lunchtime on November 24, 1975. I am seven years old and in second grade.

I just clicked open my Holly Hobby lunch box and began twisting the royal blue lid off the Thermos when my teacher, Mrs. Kanagy, answered a knock on the classroom door. She opened the door, and into the room came the gym teacher, Mr. Yoder, dressed in his two-piece warm-up suit. Mrs. Kanagy escorted Mr. Yoder to the front of the room.

"Mr. Yoder is here to announce the winner of the Thanksgiving coloring contest," she said.

Mr. Yoder moved to the center of the room, in front of the blackboard. I lifted my Thermos to my mouth and took a drink.

Did I stay within the lines? I thought.

Holding the winning turkey coloring sheet in one hand, Mr. Yoder announced, "This year's winner is Katrina Derstine!"

Putting my Thermos down, I felt all 22 pairs of eyes in the classroom turn and look at me.

"Katrina, can you come to the front of the room?" Mr. Yoder asked.

I wasn't used to having this kind of attention at my new school. I shyly walked to the front of the room, as my classmates watched.

I must have done exceptionally well staying within the lines, I thought.

I stood before Mr. Yoder, looked up, and smiled. He handed me the prize, an ice cream sandwich.

I practiced good manners and thanked him for it, but what I really wanted to say was, "I don't like ice cream sandwiches."

Every day at the end of lunch, an older student came to the classroom, selling ice cream sandwiches for 25 cents. So, having an ice cream sandwich really wasn't anything special.

After I received my "prize," I walked back to my seat.

What do I do with this prize that I don't like? I thought. *I should like ice cream sandwiches, but I don't. I can't pretend to like it. I don't want to be rude and give it to someone. I don't want to be ungrateful and throw it away.*

I wanted to play by the rules. My second-grade mind told me to go to the bathroom, which was in the back of the classroom. Once in the bathroom, I could have thrown the ice cream sandwich away, but instead I decided to flush it down the toilet. I was no longer basking in the glory of being the best colorer in the class. I was determined to hide the fact that I didn't like the prize, so I put the entire ice cream sandwich in the toilet, wrapper and all, pushed the handle, and watched, hoping for the best. It flushed.

Walking out of the bathroom, I felt happy that I "hid" the prize. Once I got back to my seat, fear set in.

What if the toilet overflows? What if water from the toilet comes spilling out from under the door? Then the janitor would come in the room and discover that my ice cream sandwich clogged the toilet.

I imagined the janitor coming out of the bathroom, holding up the ice cream sandwich wrapper and shouting with an angry tone, "Who did this?" I should've known better. The voice in my head got louder: *Grammy, my Sunday school teacher will be right: My sins will always be found out.*

For as long as I can remember, I have suffered from FOPO: Fear of Other People's Opinions.

Symptoms of FOPO

* ✳ Disempowered; unsure of yourself
* ✳ Highly self-critical
* ✳ Indecisiveness as a result of anxiousness
* ✳ Prone to perfectionism

People pleasing can start as a young child. We hide our preferences. We're taught to be good girls. We're told: Don't say no—not even no, thank you! We don't want to feel another's disappointment in us, so we try to control others' responses as a means to manage our own anxiety. Their reactions and responses feed the fear that we are not good or something is wrong with us, especially if we already believe we are not good enough.

Playing by the "rules" and being a compliant good girl was an unconscious attempt to get love and feel I belonged. I tried to control others' opinions of me to gain their approval.

Because of this fear, I wanted to belong more than I wanted to be honest about what I thought, liked, or felt. Not being honest kept me from expressing my feelings, and I was always adapting. It is like "checking" the weather and assessing the conditions in order to play by the often unspoken rules.

Feelings, stories of unworthiness, and shame can cause the fear of other people's opinions. It is the feelings that arise from feeling cut off in relationships. As adults, we feel unsafe until we do the work to begin to experience some of the love and understanding we needed as children. We relate to others in terms of how they affect our level of fear. In each of our relationships, we subconsciously ask:

✴ Does this person give me something that might alleviate my fear, such as reassurance, comfort, and company?

✴ Does this person increase my fear? Does she make me feel worse about myself? Does she see that I am afraid? Am I safe with her?

We live in our own endangered world, constantly scanning for threats. When someone criticizes us or disapproves, it throws us back in time. We feel as if we were a child who is powerless, alone, and terrified. To make matters worse, we worry that if others see we are afraid, we may be unlikeable, possibly making them reject us.

And so, we pretend to be unafraid. Yet as we pretend to be okay, we sink even more deeply into feeling separate, alone, and threatened.

When we believe something is wrong with us, we are convinced we are in danger. The very fact that we feel fear fuels shame. Our fear makes us worry we are broken or incapable. Our shame fuels more fear, and then our fear fuels more shame. It is an endless cycle.

We begin to believe that we are defined by being fearful and bad. And so, we learn to lie to avoid anger, disapproval, or judgement. To avoid these feelings, we try harder to be good, thinking it will protect us from rejection.

To heal, I needed to change the story and reframe how I viewed fear.

Journal January 2017

I gave up parts of myself to keep the peace. And what does it profit a person if they gain the world but lose their soul? My external world is peaceful, but internally it feels far from peaceful. I am a peacekeeper, not a peacemaker.

> "People who lack confidence are addicted to other people's approval."
>
> —Unknown

Your Freedom Toolkit

○ Test feedback from others; don't accept other people's opinions without testing its truth. Others are allowed to have their opinions, but their opinions don't have to change yours.

○ It's futile trying to control what other people think. We can spend less time caring about what people think of us when we realize most often others are thinking about themselves.

○ Lighten up and avoid taking yourself so seriously. Have a "this is me" kind of attitude to what others think about you. You like what you like. I like what a friend said to me as we were walking down a street one day, "Own your shit!" In other words, fear less about being too much. You do you. Remember that some people are going to like you, and other people aren't, so you might as well be you. Then, at least, you know that the people who like you truly do like you.

○ Don't shrink and/or sugarcoat your words. If you have something to say, say it. When you express yourself, it can feel like a small earthquake. The ground shakes for a time, but then it's over. With those you love and feel safe with, do not sugarcoat your words. Say what you mean. You are a human being, not a human giver. You have preferences, desires, needs, and wants. People's responses to what you think, do, or feel tell you about them. It's not about you. Their reactions give you information about who they are. Your identity is not what others think of you.

○ Were you taught not to rock the boat, or to be seen but not heard? Test the messages you were taught as a child. Are they accurate? True? Do they fit with who you want to become?

Your Freedom Toolkit

○ Befriend your feelings of fear, especially when you need to lean into difficult conversations. Important and meaningful things are scary. Being scared is normal. In scripture, the sentence "do not be afraid" is mentioned 365 times. Fear can be a teacher, an important messenger. It signals an opportunity to pay attention and to love ourselves in the moment. Ask a friend to comfort you when you are afraid.

○ Find role models who are centered in who they are. Read biographies of persons who live authentically, such as Alicia Keys, Dolly Parton, Michelle Obama, and Helen Reddy. Realize that you don't need to hustle for your worth. You were born with it.

○ Understand that no one can argue with your feelings. For example, if you say, "It feels like Wednesday." No one can argue with that. You define what Wednesday feels like to yourself. When you share your feelings, it may not feel good at first because this is not your pattern. You may feel selfish, bitchy, opinionated, or needy. Resist labeling your feelings. Feelings are information.

○ Be patient with your recovery from FOPO. Getting over FOPO is like flexing new muscles. It's about making progress, not doing it perfectly. Give yourself time to adjust as you practice expressing yourself and showing up differently.

○ List the worst things that someone could say about you. Imagine yourself in a courtroom with a piece of Plexiglas between you and the person you fear the most. Pretend that person is saying nasty things, but the words don't hit you. They just slide down the Plexiglas!

Some examples:

You're an idiot.

You're just like your mother.

Who do you think you are?

You are so selfish.

You're disgusting.

You are a horrible person.

You should be so ashamed of yourself.

What are you thinking?

Are you crazy?

Are you out of your mind?

Figure out who you are.

You're such a bitch.

You're going to hell.

You're a cheater.

You're a joke.

You're fake.

Pray: Love, please help me to see my fear as a signal to show myself grace and compassion.

Journal October 2007

Awaken me, that I may be free of fear.

Free of fear.

What would that look like?

Who would I be?

Awaken me.

"When you're healed, you wake up every morning and feel free. Free of the grip of fear. Free of caring whatever everybody else thinks. Free of feeling like you have anything to prove. Free of worrying that you're not enough. Free of self-beatings. Free of muddy confusion. Free to be unapologetically you. Free. You feel very alive! When you're healed, you may cry more than ever. But those feelings come, flood you, and release, rather than getting stuck. You know you are not alone. When you are healed, your feel deeply connected to me. You know that everything is happening in perfect harmony with a greater plan. You feel free of anxiety, because you know you are held and safe and the world is conspiring to help you walk your path with ease. It's that simple. Do you want to feel healed?"

—Your Inner Pilot Light (written by Lissa Rankin, MD)

Fear Heartplay

Fear says:
See, hear, and accept me
Welcome me
I am a special guest
Don't shut the door on me
Let me in
I have something really important to tell you
You are not broken
You made up that story
I am an important messenger
I am a signal to show yourself love
I have important things to tell you
I would leave you alone
But you have important work to do
Invite me in
When the time is right
Ask love to kick me out

Reflections

- What is your earliest memory of pleasing people?

- Rewrite a different ending to the story. What empowered action could you have done?

- What do you want to say to your frightened younger self? What comfort and reassurance do you need now?

- Write the names of five people whose opinions really matter to you. What does each person love most about you? Let those words sink in.

STEP 4

Burn the Box

"If everyone has to think outside the box,
then maybe it is the box that needs to be examined."
—*Malcolm Stillwell*

I have a blue T-shirt with white lettering that says on the front, World's Okayest Mom.

My son Jake gave me this T-shirt for my 46th birthday! Not gonna lie, it made me pause when I took the shirt out of the gift wrap.

I soon realized the truth of it. Ever since my children were born, I was trying to fit into the box society created for moms: Super Mom. The harder I tried to fit in the box, the more I felt that I failed.

The words on that T-shirt served as a reminder that I could let go of trying to squeeze myself into a box that didn't fit. There was lots of angst and frustration trying to fit in that box, until I stopped striving and chose to burn the box.

One year, at my kids' elementary school book fair, I bought a book called *Confessions of a Slacker Mom*. I read it multiple times. I needed validation that it was okay to be average, ordinary, and the "okayest" mom.

It was like I believed there was a competition for Best Mom, and

31

someday I would get a medal. But the reality is, I got a T-shirt!

For me, being the okayest mom means I am doing the best I can. I can burn the box of super mom. My mantra became:

I do enough.

I have enough.

I am enough.

I'm grateful to my son Jake for the endearing gift. Being the world's okayest mom is a worthy endeavor, and burning the box of super mom has been freeing!

People pleasing can keep us chasing an ideal. I wanted to look and be the perfect mom. For most of my adult life, I felt the conflict between being honest and keeping up appearances to please others. I overextended myself trying to cover up the parts of myself that I feared were unacceptable. Don't let anyone see your dirty laundry! Keep it all contained, neat, and tidy in a box.

My former spouse was a pastor at a large Mennonite church. I was a pastor's wife. My perceived "job" was to wear my Sunday best, be the perfect "help mate" and the epitome of a Godly woman, all the while managing four active children and silently crying in the pew as I struggled to keep up the appearance that our marriage and family were perfect. They weren't. I blew up the "perfect family" box when I asked my husband to leave our home in 2006, and we separated for a time, which in turn affected his job as a pastor.

Two of our greatest needs as humans are to be known and loved by others. Yet many people believe: If you really knew me, you wouldn't love me. There is much to explore about who you are. You are what you love, not who loves you. What if you lived without the four walls of a "box," opening your mind, body, and spirit to live a rich, full life that can't be contained to a box? Life doesn't have to be a certain way. Let yourself off the hook.

Freedom from people pleasing is creating a life where you believe you are enough without feeling like you need to behave a certain way in order to be accepted and loved. I grew up with the belief that being the same as everyone in my family would create peace and oneness. If I conformed to the beliefs of my family and church, we all would be one, be unified. Believing this was like an old Greek story where persons would be carried into the city on a cot, and when they got to the center of town, if there was some part of this person's body that didn't fit on the cot, it would be cut off. Sounds harsh, doesn't it? But in some ways, people pleasing is like amputating parts of ourselves that don't fit in the box. Recovering from people pleasing is to rediscover parts of ourselves that we cut off to cope, fit in and belong. Burn the box.

Journal September 2007

Tears are streaming down my face. I am angry at the church.

Angry at God.

Church was our life–it determined what we could and could not do.

Shoulds.

Obligations.

Compliant.

Contained.

Fear of being too much. I don't want to be the good girl. Resisting.

Grieving all that I thought was that now isn't. What does it look like to be angry at God? Can I be angry with God? Damn church–they are not getting any of my energy right now. Praying. I resist praying.

Drawn to silence.

Don't want quick-fix spirituality or others unloading their desires on me about what or how God is going to use this in my life.

Leave me alone.

I desire to develop a stronger sense of self.

Starting and beginning again with no assumptions.

Your Freedom Toolkit

○ Our lives are shaped by religious and cultural norms. I told my kids there was an order to life: graduate from high school, work, date, and get married. I feared that if they did anything out of order, it would lead to unhappiness. I don't believe that anymore. There doesn't have to be a preset order. There is no formula for life. It's liberating to realize that the most important rule is, there are no rules.

○ Assess your energy and anger. Exhaustion and resentment are signs you may be trying to fit into a box.

○ Remember that sometimes we cling to preset ways of doing something because it feels safe. Safety is an illusion. Growth happens outside of our comfort zone.

○ Test the norms. Ask yourself: What do I want? How does this fit with what I believe? Is this my truth? An important part of human development is to test the cultural and religious norms that form our personalities and lives. Life is like a Lego set. One can put the Lego set together the first time according to the beautiful diagram, but then take it apart and create one's own design, choosing what features to include the second time around.

○ Think outside the box. In a box, certain things are acceptable. Outside the box, there's a lot to explore. Let your curiosity lead you to take the lid off the box and climb out. What are you curious about? What sparks your interest?

○ List 5 to 10 things you are curious about. Set a date and time to explore an item on the list.

○ Try on and out new ways of being. Be like a child who moves freely in a room full of toys. Likewise, there is more than one ride at a amusement park, so try out many "rides!" Or test drive many "cars!"

○ Pray: I let go of thinking life should be a certain way and live with ease and freedom as life unfolds.

Be a Ripple Maker

Women stand in the center of a deep pond, surrounded by everyone we love. Every move we make has a ripple effect on the people in the pond.

If we make a small move, we create a small wave. If we make a big move, we create big waves.

Even if you're doing the healthy thing, you're making a wave. And that means someone in your pond is going to get wet.

A difference between men and women is that women tend to notice when other people are getting wet, and we feel badly, deluged by guilt.

Burning the familiar box will create ripples, but so will staying in the box. Either way, you make waves. Allow others to know the real you.

Reflections

- What box are you resisting climbing out of? What is the cost of climbing out of a box?

- Don't be afraid of being different; be afraid of being the same as everyone else. What makes you unique?

- In what way could you live more honestly? What parts of yourself do you hide?

STEP 5

Trust Yourself

"It's not your job to fix everyone, be liked all the time, do it all, please everyone, always hold it together, and be strong all the time."
—*Unknown*

One morning when I was in fifth grade, I bounced down the outside stairwell to go to my classroom at the small Christian school not far from my home. I was wearing clogs, a brown skirt, and a cream, button-down, ruffled top. The sun was bright, and I felt great because the night before I got my hair cut.

I opened the basement door that led to the dark hallway lined with lockers. I headed into my classroom, and my teacher, who was standing behind her desk, greeted me almost the minute I stepped into the classroom.

"Good morning! Did you do something different to your hair?" she quickly asked.

"Yes, I got my hair cut," I responded happily.

"Did you do something different?" she asked with a slight edge to her voice.

"I did. I parted my hair on the side."

She quickly responded, "I like the part better in the middle."

I felt like she had drilled a hole in my boat. I was no longer floating. I had the sinking feeling that I didn't look as good as I thought I did.

She knows better, I thought. *She is right. My hair does look better that way.*

For decades after that, I wore the same hairstyle, never straying from the middle part, believing that my fifth grade teacher knew best. I allowed her opinion to change what I was feeling, what I knew.

As people pleasers, we can lose our sense of self. We allow other people's beliefs and opinions to be heavy blankets that hide our truth. It can get to the point where we wonder, *What do I like? What do I think?*

We often take on false beliefs like "I don't know enough" or that we need one more course, program, or guru to deem us worthy. We hold on to the belief that other people know more than we do. We don't trust our innate wisdom and truth. Learning to trust this innate wisdom comes from listening to the most powerful and secure part of you: your wise Self or Source. Trusting ourselves requires us to get quiet and spend time alone.

Having four children and lots of friends, I avoided time alone. It was only when I was diagnosed with thyroid cancer and pregnant with my third child that I realized it was time to wake up and uncover the root of this dis-ease in my body. I wanted to get quiet.

I began a program where over the course of three years I spent one weekend a month at a spiritual retreat center. During these quiet weekends, I began to uncover my voice, which in turn helped me to trust myself.

Trusting yourself is about getting to know yourself, the unstoried self. The self without all the stories we create to help ourselves make sense of what is happening to us. Remember, there was a time as a child when we knew instinctively what to do.

Trusting yourself is like peeling away the layers of life to get to the core of who you are. It is believing you can still be like that child who smiles when happy, cries when upset, explores, discovers, falls down, and gets up. Trusting yourself is moving in the world like a free-spirited child who knows her worth and power.

Reflections

- What do you feel when you say the word *power*?
  What does personal power mean to you?

- Trusting yourself is owning your power. In what ways do
  you give away your power to others?

- Select a topic like money and begin to write about it.
  Whose voice is it? Write with your own voice.

STEP 6

Tell Your Truth

"The hardest part of being a woman is telling 'our' truth, all of it."
—Maya Angelou

Are you brave enough to awaken?

One day my friend Elke called. We met in a coaching group a year earlier. She is my age and from Germany, but she was living in Atlanta at the time. Because I have family roots in Germany, I was intrigued by her background and how it's similar to mine.

One day, Elke observed, "You are so hard on yourself. I feel like there is something else going on." She challenged me, "Go deeper in your writing." With her encouragement, I felt the desire to go deeper and tell the truth. As if eavesdropping on my Soul, I wrote what I heard. My truth spilled out.

I am afraid

Afraid I will not want to be married

Afraid I will want to move to California and be a spiritual guru

Afraid I will be misunderstood

Afraid I will be happy but alone
Afraid I will dabble in evil things
I am scared I won't get into heaven
I am scared I will take it too far
So many damn filters: cultural, religious, and family
What the hell do I think and feel?

I admitted the truth. As people pleasers, we must dig through the layers of life to uncover the truth. Image keeping and secret keeping were killing my soul. To revive my soul, honesty and truth telling were required.

In my heart, I knew facing my fears was going to be disruptive and life-changing but important in honoring and valuing myself. Why is it so hard to admit we are afraid?

We allow children to be afraid, but as adults we walk around and act as if no one is afraid. When my daughter Lydia was young, she was afraid of thunderstorms. Whenever there was a thunderstorm, she would want me to hold her. One summer, I was afraid of letting her go to a wilderness camp because I knew during the high heat of summer, storms happen. Lydia's fears didn't keep her from going.

Brené Brown, PhD, defines courage as being "brave and afraid." Lydia was courageous! I reassured her that fears are normal and that even though I wasn't there, other people would be there to take care of her, which she experienced when a big thunderstorm blew through the wilderness camp.

Overcoming people pleasing takes the same kind of courage in facing our fears. We are reassuring, comforting, and present to our children's fears, but we ignore our own fears. Our own fears need this same kind of comfort and acceptance.

I coach many adults, like myself, who were raised in emotionally repressed families, and as a result become used to denying pain, discomfort, and fear. Because of the fear of rejection and feeling unsafe, we are reluctant to share who we are. When we sense we might be rejected, it ignites strong feelings of inadequacy. Who wants to feel that? So, to avoid those feelings of fear and judgement, we do things to extremes. We overgive, overwork, overeat. Unconsciously, we protect and hide ourselves because we are afraid. We develop addictions and dependencies. We numb our fear to cope.

I continued to name my fears during the pandemic, which coincided with the dissolving of my marriage:

I am afraid to be alone

I am scared to be myself

I fear being labeled selfish

I fear being rejected

Even as I write, I am scared

I am afraid of everything I can't control

Control is a big illusion

I can't control anything

To heal from pleasing people, tell the truth. To tell the truth is to accept ourselves, warts and all, especially the afraid and scared parts of ourselves. When we accept ourselves, we acknowledge our feelings. We allow our feelings to be what they are. Feelings are information. In my awakening journey, I grew to trust that my feelings are healthy and could be trusted. Our feelings are an opportunity to explore, not to overanalyze but a chance to show ourselves compassion and accept our humanness. When we tell the truth, it is an opportunity to nurture ourselves in caring, loving ways.

Journal February 2001

Yes, I felt hurt yesterday. What should I be learning? What is it that hurts? I am restless. I want God's plan for me to come into being now. I want to have important things in my life. I want to be known. I have a longing to be known and loved for who I am.

Your Freedom Toolkit

○ Tell the truth. When we are honest, we feel freer and more at peace. When I hid the truth from myself and others, I did not feel free to be myself. I was restless, often looking for things outside of myself to change. I couldn't change anyone but myself. I grappled with the truth. It takes courage to explore the truth. The truth is I wasn't happy in my marriage. I needed to accept that truth or change it.

○ Accept that part of being human is to be afraid. It is one of the four main feelings: scared, happy, sad, and hurt.

○ When you allow yourself to feel afraid, it is a signal to show yourself some love. It is an opportunity to give yourself the love and attention you look to others to give you. Let the energy of fear pass through you. Understand that the first step of change is awareness. The second step is to act.

○ Remember that you are not alone. Tell someone you feel safe with the truth. We are wired for connection. Share your feelings with safe people in your life. When we are vulnerable with others, it creates connection, and it builds trust. When I told dear friends, "I am afraid," it was freeing. It is difficult to be comfortable in your skin if you are holding back parts of yourself in relationships. According to Matthew Kelley in his book, *The Seven Levels of Intimacy*, sharing our fears with another person is the deepest level of intimacy. When we tell the truth and share our fears, it can build deep connections with another person. It is through this connection that the pleaser stops being the helper, accommodator, and fixer and becomes vulnerable. When we are vulnerable, it creates true intimacy. A phrase that demonstrates intimacy is "in-to-me-see." To overcome pleasing others, it is important for others to know what we think, feel, and believe in order for them to know us. It is important—and we deserve the right—to be vulnerable with people who are safe. (See "Communication Tools" on page 46.)

Your Freedom Toolkit

○ Feelings are like the 88 keys on a piano. Play the full range of "keys" or feelings. All our feelings are worth playing and can create a beautiful melody! The more we tell the truth, the more alive we become as we accept our humanness. Experiencing a negative emotion is like touching a hot burner. The heat and/ or burn gives you information. So does a feeling. You can decide how long you want to keep your hand on the burner, so to speak. Acknowledge the truth.

Communication Tools

Try these communication tools with a trusted friend, using these phrases:

- "What I need from you is…"
- "I would like your support…"
- "I want to tell you…"
- "Can you…"
- "This hurts me. I need you to comfort me."
- "I am disappointed and bummed…"
- "I feel uncomfortable when you…"
- "I feel you were selfish."
- "What makes you do that?"
- "What makes you say that?"

Reflections

- At this moment, what needs my attention?

- What is happening right now? Where does it hurt? What needs my acceptance?

- Write a letter to the Divine that expresses your honest-to-God truth.

"The Voice already knows. And because the Voice knows, you are safe to tell the truth and at the same time obligated to tell the truth."

— Jennifer Connor, My Soul Pages

STEP 7

Drop into Your Heart

*"Your vision will become clear only when you look into your heart.
Who looks outside, dreams. Who looks inside, awakens."*
—Carl Jung

It is a dreary, rainy April morning, one month into a global pandemic. I am driving to my parents' house, a familiar route, a route I have driven hundreds of times, except this morning I pulled into a parking lot to gather my thoughts.

My heart is heavy. I need to drop into my heart. I am minutes away from having the most difficult conversation I ever had with my parents. I planned to share with them that I was choosing to leave my marriage.

Sitting in the car with my hand on my heart, I read out loud the declaration of freedom that I had written the day before. With tears rolling down my cheeks, I read the words that were guiding my way.

Journal April 2020
My Declaration of Freedom

I declare myself free from being held captive in this relationship where there has been so much pain that has deeply affected my soul.

I declare myself free from being held captive in this relationship that lacks true intimacy.

I declare myself free from being held captive in this relationship that has huge obstacles to overcome.

I declare myself free from being held captive in this relationship that tames my wild side.

I declare myself free from being held captive in this relationship that has been stifling.

I declare myself free from being held captive in this relationship that has been unhealthy in its codependency.

What price will I pay for this freedom? For this new identity?

I am willing to be homeless.

I am willing to have my family shame me, be angry, hurt me, and bad-mouth me.

I am ok if my kids will be angry.

I want my children to see a woman who freely loves and is loved.

I want them to see a woman who is fully alive, fully human-not a robot.

I want them to see me thrive and their father thrive.

I want them to live free and never feel like they need to settle.

I want them to see a woman who is no longer
betraying herself.

I want them to see me return to being my true self.

Prior to stopping at the park, my mind was spinning, trying to figure out how this conversation would go. I needed to drop into my heart in the moment and allow myself to anchor into the truth of one of my favorite verses, "Be still and know that I am God." My mind wanted to try to figure out how the upcoming conversation would go. What if…? What then…?

As a people pleaser, I constantly played and replayed conversations with people. My mind constantly chattered, always trying to figure things out. Especially going through a divorce, I had to stop trying to figure out things in my mind. I had to surrender control. Leaving my marriage was going to take courage to deal with others' disappointment with my choices. I had to get comfortable with being uncomfortable.

I found the best way to do this was to drop into my heart. Dropping into my heart helped me to be present in the moment. Putting my hand on my heart was symbolic of dropping into my heart. When uncomfortable, dropping into my heart helped me to connect with my body. It is a moment to say, "The past is over, the future is too scary, and the safest place to be is right here, in this moment."

Change is hard. Recovering from people pleasing will require showing up in new ways. Dropping into your heart is a way to stay centered and grounded in your heart's desire.

There are significant health benefits to dropping into your heart, where you can observe your breath and feel your beating heart. Regularly dropping into your heart by paying attention to your breath can help regulate your nervous system, decrease stress levels, and lower your heart rate and blood pressure. Over time, it can also help reduce depression and even ease chronic pain.

That day in the parking lot, I had to center myself in the moment and notice Presence with me.

Your Freedom Toolkit

○ When we people please, we keep the peace with others, but often we don't feel peace internally. Dropping into your heart allows you to find a place of inner peace and stillness when "rocking the boat" like before and after stepping into new, challenging conversations.

○ In Hebrew, "breath" is another word for "spirit." Take the word "Yahweh," another name for God and with your hand on your heart, breathe in "Yah" and on the exhale breathe out "Weh." Or say quietly to yourself: "I am breathing in, and I am breathing out" with each inhale and exhale.

○ Dropping into your heart is an act of mindfulness. Being present helps to create rich and meaningful experiences, which is what life is about. When we develop mindfulness, we can respond rather than react to triggers that cause us to people please.

○ Within us is a place of unconditional love, a place of acceptance and love. We can go to this place hundreds of times a day. Paying attention to our breath is a silent prayer and gives new meaning to "praying without ceasing." As you drop into your heart, it is an opportunity to listen to Source, which offers reassurance, comfort, and strength.

○ Listen to the longings of your heart. It's not that we don't know what we want, often we can't admit what we want.

○ Pray: Love, in this moment, calm me so my strength and confidence can be restored.

"When you can be present, you will know the real Presence.
I promise this is true."
—Richard Rohr

Breath Heartplay

Breathe

Relax your jaw

Relax your shoulders

Let go of striving

Let me be your guide

The internal guidance system

Leading you to the next right thing

Stop trying to figure things out

Stop being mean to yourself

It is self-abuse

Trust

Believe me when I say

Someday you will look back and ask,

How did I get here?

Allow

Allow your big life to unfold

Allow yourself to roar

Be the spiritual person that you are

Breathe

Reflections

• Where in your body do you feel tension?

• Reflect on the beauty of the present moment where you have safety, control, and your own approval. What are three good things that are happening right now?

• What is something you are trying to figure out? Can you let it go for 30 seconds, 1 minute, 5 minutes, or more?

"Whenever you feel unsettled, go inside to that place of peace, fullness, well-being, and love. Reside there and center yourself in me. The externals are not reality and will pass. Rest in my peace, love, and joy. Trust me and trust in my divine timing. There is much to arrange."
—Janet Connor

STEP 8

Write Your Way to Freedom

"To be empowered as a woman is to have a soul of one's own, the ability or means to voice it, and the courage to voice it all."
—Sue Monk Kidd

One day during college, when I was home on a break, my mom read my journal. Later that night at dinner, when it was my mom and me, she confronted me about an experience I had at college, which she had read about in my journal. Friends have told me this would have stopped them from ever writing again.

Not me. I was glad she read it because it was freeing not to have to hide the shame of that experience anymore. We could finally talk about it. As a people pleaser, I often hid my true self—especially from the people closest to me.

I don't fear others reading my journals because they will find someone who is trying to navigate life! My logic is that if someone chooses to read my journal, they will have to deal with what they discover. It is liberating because I know as a people pleaser hiding, protecting, and keeping "secrets" is exhausting.

Have you ever tried to keep a beach ball under water? It takes a lot of energy, brute strength even, to keep the buoyant ball from popping up and out of the water.

Keeping feelings of shame, guilt, and fear under wraps is like holding a beach ball underwater. It takes a lot of energy. Your feelings, just like that ball, want to come up and out.

It can be difficult to let those feelings out, especially feelings that you've held in for a long time. There are several ways you can let your feelings out, such as talking with a friend or a counselor. Another way is to become an observer of your life, reflecting upon and writing what you notice and feel.

I've been a reflector and writer of my life since I was in grade school, fourth grade to be exact, when I started writing in my Ziggy diary.

Perhaps I was inspired by my grandmother, who kept a five-year diary by her bed. Even after grade school, I continued to write. My Ziggy diary long filled up, I began writing in spiral notebooks. I often wrote during my high school classes, pretending that my journal writing was diligent note taking!

Today, I store my journals—my "life" in writing—in a plastic bin in my closet. At any moment, I can pull out a journal and "taste" my life for a second time.

Recently, at a networking event, we were asked to share about a time when we felt really listened to. Many of the participants—including me—couldn't recall a time in recent months when we felt heard. How sad for all of us—yet how powerful is the realization that we can listen to ourselves.

It's invaluable to have someone listen to us, but to reflect and write is a way to listen to ourselves. We can blame others for not being there for us, but we often don't listen to ourselves. When you write, you demonstrate to yourself that you are worthy of being listened to. At the same time, you deepen your friendship with yourself.

When I start to write, there is a lot of mind noise and chatter. But after a few minutes of writing, another voice starts to emerge—a tender, accepting, grace-filled, loving voice. I named that voice Gentle Breeze, and I also call it God.

When you pick up your pen to write, it's like telling your soul that you are ready to listen. I hope you will begin to hear a loving, kind, empathetic voice that is tender, like a dear friend.

Taking time to write provides space to refocus and recenter.

Self-expression is so important for our health and well-being as people pleasers because the quieter we become, the more we can access our voice. Writing is like eavesdropping on your soul, tuning in to listen, and hearing what it wants to say. We tune in and work to accept what is, letting go of what was, and having faith in what will be.

Our souls love the truth. When we take time to reflect and write, it helps us take responsibility for our choices. In essence, it improves our "respond-ability"! We are not reacting to life's challenges, but we are making a choice in how we will respond. The key to change is self-awareness. Writing and self-reflection are opportunities to pay attention to what we are learning when we show up in new ways. Listening is one of the oldest forms of healing, but it requires someone to listen. When we write, we heal as we listen to ourselves. Writing is a courageous act. Getting rid of deeply embedded people-pleasing habits requires courage. Writing is a path to find your voice, which in turn improves your well-being.

"I write of that journey of becoming as free as God."
—*Mirabai, I Write of That Journey.*

Journal February 2018

Not everyone will like you

Fact

You give away your power

When you try so hard to be liked

Be yourself

Do you know how to do that?

Let me tell you

Listen

Write more

You are who you are when you are with yourself

Space

Silence

See what comes up

No plan

No editing

No holding back

It's the recipe

Listen

Appreciate

Acknowledge

Your Freedom Toolkit

○ Schedule time once a day, or at least once a week, to reflect and write. Join a writing group if you need accountability. Make a bulleted list of your thoughts. Listen to yourself like you would listen to a friend. Ask yourself, what can you celebrate, appreciate, or acknowledge about yourself?

○ Store your journal in a secret place or just leave it out as a visual reminder to write.

○ Buy a blank book or notebook, grab some blank sheets of paper, or start a new "note" on your computer or phone.

○ If you don't like to write using pen and paper, create a Google doc or use journaling apps such as 5-Minute Journal, Penzu, or Grid Diary.

○ Write what you see around you. Listen. Wait. Write about a meaningful moment. A sad moment. What do you notice? What do you wish was different about this experience?

○ *New York Times* bestselling author Elizabeth Gilbert starts her journal entries with the words "Letter from Love." Notice how kindly Love speaks to you. Consider adopting a similar format to your entries, writing letters to yourself from yourself.

○ Write for as much or as little time as you want. Don't force it.

○ Avoid censoring yourself. Get the words out of your head and onto the page—whatever emotion(s) they evoke.

○ Write with ease. Explore qualities such as peace, creativity, and freedom. Write what those qualities mean to you.

○ Express appreciation to yourself. Don't wait for others to appreciate you. Write some journal entries beginning with, "I appreciate that you…"

○ Break some rules. These societal rules don't apply when journaling:

- "Think before you speak."
- "If you don't have anything nice to say, don't say anything at all."
- "Don't talk back."

○ In addition to writing things that happened in the past, you can also use writing as a tool to prepare for the future. For example, if you have an important conversation coming up, write down what you want to say. If you write your thoughts down, you are more likely to say them.

Reflections

- Like a doctor, ask yourself, "What hurts?" Write a script that will help you to heal.

- Or like a mother, ask yourself, "What do you need?"

- Or like a therapist, ask "What's going on?"

"The truth will set you free but first it will piss you off."
—Gloria Steinem

STEP 9

Break Up with Disapproval

"Summing it all up, friends, I'd say you'll do best by filling your minds and meditating on things true, noble, reputable, authentic, compelling, gracious—the best, not the worst; the beautiful, not the ugly; things to praise, not things to curse."
—Phil. 4:8

I woke up happy on a cold day in November, my 10th birthday. I reached over the chair in my bedroom and pulled the shades up on my corner windows. I had a feeling it was going to be a good day.

I wanted to look my best, so I decided to wear one of my favorite outfits. I wore my Sears plaid jeans and a white belt with a short-sleeved navy top. I stood in front of the antique oak dresser in my bedroom and combed my long, blond hair, smiling at myself. I felt beautiful.

I left my room and walked down the hallway to the dining room. When I walked into the room, my sister, who is four years older than me, was sitting at the table. She looked up and without hesitation asked, "Who do you think you are? Farrah?"

I froze.

I grew up in the '70s. My sister was talking about Farrah Fawcett, the sex symbol who was the star of the popular TV show *Charlie's Angels*.

"Who do you think you are?" are words that stayed with me for a long time. I don't fault my sister for saying that. If she had said it to one of her friends, it may have been received differently. But to an impressionable 10-year-old, being Farrah was being "too much!"

I grew up with verses from the Bible drilled into me like, "Pride comes before the fall" or "Don't think of yourself more highly than you ought." I wanted to be a good girl. I never wanted to feel too good about myself. I didn't want to disappoint God or make others uncomfortable.

Years later, when I would express myself in relationships, those words came back, "Who do you think you are to have needs, wants, desires?" I confused false pride with having a healthy self-esteem.

If people pleasing is an onion and one peels back the layers, I believe at its core there are feelings of low self-worth. My feelings of unworthiness made me feel I needed to earn *other people's* love. This lack of self-worth made me highly disapproving and critical of myself when I didn't get the love I needed. My critical mindset sat on the top of a mountain of unexpressed needs, disappointments, and desires. As people pleasers, we need to break up with disapproval and the critical spirit we have toward ourselves. It is like we are constantly saying to ourselves, "Who do you think you are?"

Marianne Williamson's poem called "Deepest Fear" speaks to this when she writes, "Our deepest fear is that we are powerful beyond measure, it is our light not our darkness that most frightens us ...you are a child of God, you playing small doesn't serve the world."

Not approving of ourselves is a way to play small. It keeps us from experiencing our limitless potential and power. Our egos like when we play small. Bringing forth our light, or becoming our true self, is a courageous act. It may seem easier to stay small with our disapproving words than to be fabulous, own our talent, and great beauty. It is not healthy. The world needs you, not some other version of you. Embracing our light means we are growing, changing, and moving forward. Consider it a compliment if someone says that you are full of yourself. It may inspire them to let their light shine brighter.

To break off with disapproval is to rest in being who you are, to shine. We grow up with messages that keep us from accepting ourselves as the divinely crafted, exquisite masterpieces that we are.

People pleasers can be extremely hard on themselves. A lot of my suffering was a result of not having more grace, compassion, and acceptance for who the Divine made me to be. Instead I was often contorting myself into someone who would be deemed more acceptable.

I believe when we grow in having more acceptance of who we are and return to that childlike belief that we are good and whole just as we are, we show up in the world as our most alive, true selves.

Growing up religious, I wanted to do things right and be good. The message "Your sins you will find you out!" created a gloom-and-doom judging view of God, which I have been battling for a long time.

Slowly, the Doom-and-Gloom view of God changed to the Sunshine God. As I sat in quiet, in the glow of Sunshine God, my self-doubt began to melt away. God, like the sun, is an ever-present, loving awareness that shines grace, compassion, and rays of acceptance to my spirit.

I sit and enjoy the feeling of this approval, which heals the need to people please.

"The Lord your God is in your midst, a mighty one who will save; he will rejoice over you with gladness; he will quiet you by his love; he will exult over you with loud singing."

—*Zephaniah 3:16 (ESV)*

Approval Heartplay

I am breaking up with
Disapproval
Obsessive
Controlling
Demeaning
The constant chatter is
Too much
She never has anything nice to say
She keeps me in a cage
The cage of my own judgement
I am never good enough
I don't do enough
I don't have enough
Today
I choose to marry approval
For no reason at all
She loves me
Minute by minute
She says
There is nothing wrong with me
She showers me with love
Holds me in love
The key labeled *love*
Opened the cage
Today
I choose approval
Approval
The leader
I longed for

Your Freedom Toolkit

○ Find an image of your younger self and put it in a place where you see it frequently. Decide not to utter a single mean word to this younger self who still lives within. See your own disapproval as self-abuse. Do no harm to yourself in thought or speech.

○ Make a list of 100 things you've accomplished and/or like about yourself that you can celebrate.

○ Be kind. Treat yourself with the respect and honor you would show a friend. Find a mentor or friend to hold you accountable as you grow in having the courage to accept yourself.

○ Create a "ta-da" list at the end of the day, acknowledging and giving yourself approval for experiences, activities, and things you accomplished!

○ Avoid comparing yourself to others. Comparison creates self-doubt and is the thief of joy!

○ When you are being critical of yourself, try to understand why. Being critical is a behavior; it's a form of anger. Ask yourself: *Am I hurt, sad, or mad?* Address the root feeling. If you are hurt, how can you feel better? If you are disappointed, how can you feel better?

○ Breathe, feel the tension, soften. Think of any disapproving thoughts as a signal to show yourself more compassion and grace.

○ In Sunday School, I learned the fruits of Spirit: love, joy, peace, patience, kindness, and goodness. I was taught if I demonstrated these "fruits," it would be a sign of living a Spirit-filled life. The greatest challenge was being gentle, loving, and kind with myself—which I wasn't taught in Sunday School.

Reflections

- Describe one to three things you have a hard time accepting about yourself.

- What ways would your life be different if you fully accepted yourself?

- What keeps you from giving yourself approval for no reason?

Journal March 2020

You have a Choice. Decide.

No	Yes
suffering	being
angry	awake
fear	wonder
restriction	surrender
disapproval	responsible
small	engaged
judging	present
closed	playful
warring	ease
hard	approval
doing	curious
striving	love
problems	safe
fake	trusting
scared	vulnerable
hurt	soft
straining	creative
striving	vitality
attaining	joyful
needy	satisfied
grasping	content
hate	inspired

STEP 10

Make Play a Priority

"She's a little weird, but she seems to be enjoying herself."
—*Unknown*

Full moons turn me on. A full moon reminds me to play. In 2009, after dinner, I went outside to dump the compost bucket out behind the garage. As soon as I stepped out the back door, I noticed the moon. On the way back, I got an idea. I opened the back door and went up the two steps into the kitchen.

"Girls, let's go!" I hollered. "Get in the car! We're going moon dancing!"

My girls didn't question their mama. They know I can be a little woo-woo at times.

We turned right out of the driveway. I drove to the only open space I knew in Perkasie, Pennsylvania.

I don't remember what we talked about on the way, but I felt excitement.

I turned left into the parking lot at the end of the walking trail. The moon was bright out in this open field, away from the houses packed in the borough.

We got out and ran halfway up the hill. Then we began twirling and dancing in the moonlight.

In the darkness, we felt free and alive—two young girls not inhib-

ited to move, and their mama alive in her spirit. We connected with the great globe of light that makes the ocean tides pull and offers a little light in the darkness.

That would be the beginning of many more moon dances. The girls eventually became old enough to realize where we danced, exclaiming, "We danced in that park?"

When they were little, they had no sense of what space their mama had taken them to.

The last moon dance I did with one of my daughters, now 17, was last year. I picked her up from youth group, and as we pulled out of the church parking lot, the moon hung low.

"Look at the moon!" my daughter and I said, almost in unison. With a giddiness in my voice, I said, "We're going moon dancing."

My daughter didn't argue. This time she drove the car! She turned left out of the church parking lot, then right, and then another left to what was once an obscure park to her. We were alone at the park after dark—just a mama and her teen daughter, twirling in the dark, feeling awake, alive, and free.

Back when this ritual began, my girls didn't own cell phones to capture the moment, but this time this middle-aged mom was captured on Snapchat. My daughter saw her mom once again living her best life by being in the moment, twirling, hugging trees, and taking great pleasure in the full moon.

The moon brings out my playful side. For many years, as a people pleaser, I knew what my children liked to do for fun, but my playful side was buried under the layers of life.

I became acutely aware of how deep I had buried my fun, playful side one day after my son Jake was born and a college friend came to visit.

"What do you like to do for fun?" my friend asked.

It took years before I could fully answer that question. In 2010, I decided to make play and fun a priority. My children were ages 15, 13, 11, and 8. At this stage in my parenting, I had given and written my kids lots of permission slips to go on field trips and playdates. I decided it was finally time to allow myself to experience more play. I wanted to reignite my playfulness. After all, I started out my professional career as a health and physical education teacher. Play was important to me. I had a desire to encourage others to make play a lifelong habit.

As people pleasers, we think we have to be on call 24/7. This leads to burnout and feeling overwhelmed and resentful.

Being in a state of play where we are led by curiosity helps us to reconnect with parts of ourselves that are buried under the layers of life. Play allows us to be completely human—our most alive selves.

Making play a priority is an opportunity to just be—to give up the doing and have a space to remember who you are. When we people please, there's a strong tendency to lose our sense of self. We ignore our legitimate needs, and we lose focus on what is important to us. It is restorative and frivolous and a great antidote to stress when we play.

Making time for fun, playful activities is not about the activity or experience, but it is rather a state of mind. How can I bring a playful spirit to an activity? It is not about the "doing," which comes naturally to the people pleaser. It is about being. When we can take time to "be," our being then informs doing the next thing. People pleasers need to be reminded we are human "beings" not human doings.

When we have space to be, like when we play, we notice we have more choice around what we do. As I made play a priority, I realized that I came back to the same circumstances and/or needs of my family. They hadn't changed while I was gone, but I had a different attitude and more energy to manage a home, family, and all that goes with it.

Your Freedom Toolkit

○ Schedule a playdate with yourself. Spend time as you want to, go window shopping, see what you are drawn to. Spending time alone allows you to make all the decisions. You are who you are when you are with yourself.

○ Protect your playtime and alone time. Defend dates with yourself as if you are keeping a date with a friend.

○ Scan your life like a person with a metal detector who scans a beach for treasures, and listen for beeps of joy! Notice what speaks to you.

○ Initiate playdates with friends or your partner/spouse. Go to places that inspire joy and creativity in you.

○ Join clubs and meet-up groups with people who have similar interests. Be curious. Explore new things and experiences.

○ How do you rate on a play meter? Think of a scale of 1 through 10, with 10 very playful and 1 not at all playful. Where do you fall?

○ Pray: Thanks for making me smile.

"We don't stop playing because we grow old.
We grow old because we stop playing."
—George Bernard Shaw

Reflections

• What turns you off? What turns you on?

• What holds you back from being more playful?

• Create a "play list" of 10 to 15 things you enjoy doing.

• Fill in the blank: Wouldn't it be crazy if____.

• Answer: I think it would be awesome if_____.

"Life is a game; play it."
—Mother Teresa

STEP 11

Tolerate Less

"We cannot simultaneously set a boundary and take care of another person's feelings."
—Melody Beattie

Last year, I was watching a high school basketball game between my kids' high school and a neighboring rival team. When a player on the other team fouled one of our star players, the student section called the P-Block, stood up, pointed fingers at the player, and started yelling, "You can't do that, you can't do that!"

As a people pleaser, I tolerated a lot. In recovery, my therapist said, "You need to move the line of what you tolerate." In my journey of awakening, I started to stand up for myself. Like the P-Block student section, I said to people in my life, "You can't do that, you can't do that!"

I tolerated a lot because I believed others would eventually *see* my frustration and hurt, and they would change. Guess what? They didn't. That never works. We can't change anyone; we can only change ourselves.

I started by changing my actions, and I began tolerating less, drawing some lines.

In the game of basketball, a player gets five fouls. In the game of life, a person must decide how many chances they will give to other people. A dear friend said to me, "You either need to accept the situation or change it."

As I changed, I realized I could be kind and loving toward others while creating limits that honor myself. Honoring and respecting myself looks like telling others, "This doesn't work for me. Can we talk?"

Relationships are about negotiating. Of course, both parties need to come to the table to negotiate. I began to see that if someone is upset when a line is drawn, they are benefiting the most from my lack of boundaries.

We tolerate something for years because it is scary to draw the line, especially if we get used to relating to another person in a certain way. Tolerating less means you're changing the dance. It's a new dance. No one knows the footwork. It feels clumsy, awkward, and out of sync.

If both parties are willing, patient, and gracious, the new dance steps can be learned as each person honors the other person's limits. Like dancing, it's a new rhythm and pattern. With time and the practice of limit setting, the new dance will become more comfortable.

The old dance might have been safe and comfortable, but that doesn't mean it was healthy.

Behind every frustration is a desire. I started to pay attention to my desires.

Our helping and pleasing can seem harmless, but when our helping becomes enabling it can keep others from becoming fully, capable humans. As I began my recovery journey, I became aware of how anxious and sensitive I was to others' emotions and how desperately I wanted to avoid their negative feelings. In order to avoid those feelings, I became "overly" accommodating, which led to resentment. One day, I told my son in frustration, "You have a pretty nice life. I do so much for you."

"I never asked you to do all that," he replied.

He was right. As pleasers, we can be on autopilot, overly helpful.

We want others to step up, but first we need to step back and find ways to calm our own anxiousness about the situation. In essence, we need to stay in our lane and ask ourselves, *Is my helping really helping?*

Generally, I believe pleasers like to be needed, and in turn, being needed feels like worthiness. If my identity is in being a helper and I stop helping or don't feel needed, then I have a bigger question to answer: Who am I apart from my helpfulness?

"Daring to set boundaries is about having the courage to love ourselves even when we risk disappointing others."
—Brené Brown, PhD

Your Freedom Toolkit

○ Make it a goal to disappoint one person a day. Lean into the discomfort of a hard conversation rather than becoming resentful.

○ Tell people close to you that you are getting a "PhD" in setting limits, so they understand you are practicing a new skill. Remember if they get upset about your boundary, they may be benefitting the most from your lack of boundaries.

○ Recognize ways you may be doing for others what they are capable of doing for themselves. If you step back, instead of worrying about how they'll manage the challenge, wonder instead. For example, "I wonder how he will figure out how to do that."

○ Be mindful that in the process of allowing another to manage a situation, they're learning new skills that they wouldn't have learned otherwise if you would've taken over.

○ Ask yourself, *What is my limit?* In track and field, a high jumper needs to jump over a bar. The bar is moved up in increments. Likewise, as a pleaser, ask yourself how high will you jump for others.

○ Once you set the bar, let the chips fall where they may. Allow other people to pick up the chips. As pleasers, we've taught others around us that we're the only ones capable of picking up the pieces!

○ Tell someone when a need is not being met. "I need empathy." "I need you to validate my feelings."

○ People grow through hard things. When we allow another to be responsible for their "stuff" at first it may be uncomfortable for them. As pleasers, we're sensitive to other people's feelings, and we can be accommodating to protect others from facing difficult situations and/or reality. They may experience hardship, but the hardship could be the very thing they need to grow. In turn, we grow by setting limits to what we tolerate.

○ Be clear. Don't sugarcoat your words. Being clear is kind to ourselves and others.

Conversation Prompts

If you choose to _____, I won't be able to communicate with you.

I am not willing to do that, but I am willing to _____.

I am afraid to tell you this because I am afraid you will dismiss what I feel.

Can you help?

As of today, I will no longer be responsible for making _____ happen.

I feel hurt when you don't consider me in making decisions. I need to be included.

Allow Heartplay

I allow myself to say no

I allow myself to honor my needs, unapologetically

I allow myself to evolve, grow, and change

I allow myself to be my true self

Reflections

• What frustrates you? What do you want?

• What conversation do you need to lean into?

• What are your limits?

STEP 12

Reinvigorate Yourself

*"Don't ask yourself what the world needs. Ask yourself what
makes you come alive and go do that because what this world needs
is people who are fully alive."*
—Howard Thurman

On July 4th, I walked into the fenced-in pool area at a retreat center
in the Poconos. I hadn't seen Katie, my daughter and an employ-
ee at the center, in over a month. When I walked in, I saw her directly
across from the entrance on the other side of the pool.

I walked down toward the edge of the pool on the concrete side-
walk, between the toddler pool filled with little tykes and their care-
givers who were sitting on the edge and the larger pool where teenage
boys were throwing a ball.

I rounded the last corner before Katie saw me, and then she began
walking toward me. When she got close enough to me, she reached up
and touched the brim of my hat.

"Hey, Mom, I didn't recognize you," she said. "You look like you just
spent two weeks traveling in Greece."

I smiled as we embraced. Inwardly, I loved that she thought I
looked like a world traveler. She spent time traveling in Greece. She

knew what Greek women looked like. I liked that she didn't recognize me. I felt chic and happy I chose that particular outfit.

Prior to our embrace, I was back in my parents' camper with its indoor bathroom and slideouts, having a debate with myself about whether I should wear the sleek, thin, off-white tunic that barely covered my bum with its one-piece bathing suit underneath or wear the deemed-more-appropriate Christian retreat camp attire: athletic shorts and a t-shirt. I thought and questioned. Should I tone down my look so I don't make someone uncomfortable? Wearing my bikini under my tunic wasn't an option, because at this camp, all women were required to wear one-piece bathing suits.

I love the light tan, wide-brimmed hat with its small tie around the inside of the rim that Katie tipped when she saw me. One early morning the previous summer at Wildwood Crest, while my other daughter, Lydia, was sleeping, I walked two blocks to a clothing shop. I set out that morning to buy a hat and tunic which, on this Independence Day, made a mom unrecognizable to her daughter.

I bought the hat and tunic that day to complete my beach outfit because I wanted to go more frequently. Lydia and I both agreed we liked the beach. The rest of the family preferred the woods, so short getaway weekends tended to be about camping and packing the "house" in the back of the minivan or truck.

For some time, I had anticipated that beach weekend with Lydia. It was the weekend I was going to wear a bikini for the first time.

At 50, it was time to embrace my femininity and curves and celebrate my beautiful body that birthed four children, ran countless miles, and housed my most prized possession—my heart. I was letting go of feeling responsible for other people's choices.

Early in my life I decided to adhere to a scripture passage that says, "Do not cause another person to stumble." In my attempt to be deemed good, I wanted to play by the rules, so I held to my belief for half a century that somehow by wearing a modest one-piece bathing suit I could shield another person from stumbling or sinning. I let go of the long-held belief that I was responsible for someone else's choices.

So that weekend at the beach, I walked the beach in my bikini. I felt

so free! I tried not to beat myself up for not wearing a bikini sooner. I wondered, *Why have I wasted so much time and energy trying to control what other people think or feel about me*? It's futile.

As I walked the shoreline, I noticed my shadow as I practiced the "walk." A few weeks earlier, I had flown to a conference in Atlanta, Georgia. The conference was called the Art of the Feminine Presence. I was owning my feminine side and the invigorating feeling I felt when I was in touch with that side, feeling sensual and embracing the gift of my body. That day on the beach, I felt like a little girl who plays dress up, trying on different ways of being. Except I wasn't pretending—I was a 50-year-old woman with wants, needs, and desires. The biggest desire was to embrace who Love created me to be, letting go of old conditioning and beliefs. Choosing to let go of the belief that I might become too wild and free, perhaps even traveling far from "home" to exotic places like Greece!

On the beach that day, I ended up with a bad case of sunburn on the unblemished baby-like skin on my stomach. The pain of the burn reminded me that I am responsible for my choices. It's my life! I will keep playing dress up.

What are you doing when you feel your most alive self? To reinvigorate yourself is to decide who you want to become, and to make choices aligned with who you want to be—that is intentional living! Don't let life happen to you. Infuse your life with experiences that make you feel the way you want to feel. When we are our most alive selves, we are our most true selves. There is no hiding, pretending, or trying to prove we are good, or good enough. Reinvigorate yourself by paying attention to what makes you feel alive. The world needs the most alive version of you!

Your Freedom Toolkit

○ Keep discovering new things about yourself. You have layers. You are not just one-dimensional. Every day is an opportunity to grow and learn something new about yourself.

○ Do something for the first time. The older we get, the fewer firsts we have. Experiences or firsts help us get out of ruts.

○ Deepen your friendship with yourself. Treat yourself as if you are getting to know yourself for the first time.

○ Rather then feeling resentment for feeling stuck, lean into the discomfort of doing more things that make you feel the way you want to feel. Do you want to feel more vitality? Joy? Freedom? Peace?

○ Make a list of things you want. Let yourself think big. Choose one goal from the list and commit to bringing it to fruition.

○ Own who the Divine made you to be. Love doesn't start when someone loves you; it starts with you loving yourself first. People pleasing is a facade. People don't see you; they see a version of someone else.

○ Lean in to uncomfortable situations. If you are uncomfortable, it is a sign you are growing. Discomfort is the admission ticket to a meaningful life.

○ Pray: Thank you for love, the greatest superpower in the world.

Reflections

- What does the word *reinvigorate* mean to you?

- What are you doing when you feel your most alive self? Describe in detail.

Let Go Heartplay

Stay in my lane

I am not responsible for their well-being

Stay in my lane

I am not responsible if they have a happy life

I let go

I am responsible for myself

I cannot change anyone

Stay in my lane

I cannot control anyone

Be present

Be honest

Allow

This is a start

Stay in my lane

ACKNOWLEDGMENTS

Thank you to my children, Micah, Katie, Jacob, and Lydia, who are my greatest teachers. They were the first to hear I was writing a book and the most supportive! Katie and Lydia, thanks for your feedback, especially on the cover.

Mom and Dad, thank you for the hugs, meals, and company during this season of writing. Your unwavering support in everything I have done in my life has been such a gift to me and my children.

To my therapists, coaches, spiritual directors, and teachers who have been a part of my healing journey, thank you Karen Williamson, Dr. William McCollaum, Wayne Schzanenbach, Pam Asks, Patricia Hickey, Sandra Drescher Lehman, and Jennifer Schelter. Thanks to the teachers who mentored me from afar, whose work I deeply respect and admire: Oprah, Glennon Doyle, Sarah Bloudin, Sue Monk Kidd, and Paula D'Arcy.

Heartfelt thank you to the team at Bright Communications, especially my editor, Jennifer Bright, who encouraged me and held me accountable to making my dream to be an author come true!

Shout out to my dear friends who have been by my side and who have inspired me to fly! Thank you to my monthly writing friends, the Story Studio, who provided encouragement and support as we wrote our stories.

Last but not least, thanks to my Creator, who calls me out to play and to be more than I could ever imagine!

TRINA STUTZMAN

ABOUT THE AUTHOR

TRINA STUTZMAN is a holistic life coach, author, and speaker. With more than 20 years of personal and professional experience, Trina wants individuals to live their lives freely and intentionally.

As a former corporate wellness coach, health advisor, and lay minister, Trina combines all of her expertise and passions to help individuals. She navigates them through taking a full-scope inventory of all the different roles they are playing in their lives and get to the root of who they actually are: powerful and limitless. Trina helps individuals identify the root source of their suffering and stress, recognize their choices, implement a plan for change, and begin to live a life that they love.

Trina has traversed her own wildly transformational soul journey. From the outside, Trina's life looked pretty amazing: She was living as a pastor's wife, a busy sports mom, and a working professional. She was thoroughly consumed with everyone else's happiness but her own. It took a diagnosis of cancer for Trina to wake up to her self-sacrificing behaviors and take a personal inventory of her own. She took a deep spiritual dive, which led her to three years of study at the Kairos School of Spiritual Formation. Soon after completing the program, she experienced a very public separation from her husband and changed course with her previous pastoral aspirations. As Trina took back her own health and wrestled with a shattered public image, she started to listen to her intuition and began accessing the true version of her authentic self.

In 2009, Trina started her own coaching practice to help other women realize they too cannot pour from an empty cup. Trina is a sought-after life coach, public speaker, thought leader, and reiki master.

Trina holds credentials through Stephen Ministry International and International Coaching Federation and holds a Certificate in Family Business Advising from the Family Firm Institute.

When she's not coaching and empowering others, she can be found living the life that she loves and spending time with her four children in Bucks County, Pennsylvania.

Free Newsletter

Join the movement of recovering people pleasers and receive a free resource providing insights, tips, and the latest happenings in Trina's world.

Personal Coaching

Need a guide by your side to help you live intentionally? Trina is not a guru on a mountaintop, but someone whose healing journey is the hope she offers to others. As a result of working with Trina, you will gain confidence and clarity to make changes to live the life you love.

Recovery Group for People Pleasers

Connect with others who desire to stop putting themselves on the back burner. Are you ready to take back your life? In this recovery group, you will learn from others, gain the confidence to make changes, and grow in becoming more of your true self.

Book Study

Gather a group of friends to grow and learn together! Trina is available to join a gathering and provide specially designed RPP (Recovering People Pleaser) merchandise for groups.

Need a speaker for your event?

Trina has experience presenting at women's events, retreats, church services, community colleges, forums, lunch and learns, webinars, and other venues. She is available to speak at corporate wellness days, breakout sessions, discussion panels, workshops, in-person and online learning opportunities, and retreats.

12 Steps to Overcome People Pleasing Course – Coming Soon!

Connect with Trina on social media:

Facebook: Trina Stutzman Coaching
Linked In: Trina Stutzman
Instagram: Trina Stutzman Coaching
Website: Trinastutzman.com